AGAINST THE POWERS

JIM WILSON

Tyndale House
Publishers, Inc.
Wheaton, Illinois

ACKNOWLEDGMENTS

Credit is hereby given to the following publications from which quotations have been taken in this book:

Memoirs of Field Marshall Montgomery, by Bernard Law Montgomery, World Publishing Company, 1958.

The *Military Classics series,* The Stackpole Company:
Jomini's Art of War, by Lt. Col. J.D. Hittle, USMC.
Principles of War, by General Karl von Clausewitz, edited by Hans W. Gatzke.
The Art of War, by Sun Tzu, edited by Thomas R. Phillips, translated by Lionel Giles.
Surprise, by General Waldemar Erfurth, translated by Dr. Stefan T. Possony and Daniel Vilfroy.

Way of a Fighter, by Maj. Gen. Claire Chennault, Putnam's and Coward-McCann. Copyright, 1949, by Claire Lee Chennault.

Allenby, A Study in Greatness, by Sir Archibald Percival Wavell, Oxford University Press.

Born to Reproduce, by Dawson Trotman, Good News Broadcasting Association, Inc.

Total Christian War, by Howard Guinness, Children's Special Services Mission, London, England.

This new revised edition published by Tyndale House Publishers, Inc., by arrangement with the author. Library of Congress Catalog Card Number 79-66811. ISBN 0-8423-0043-0, paper. Copyright © 1980 by James I. Wilson. All rights reserved. Printed in the United States of America. Second printing, March 1981.

CONTENTS

FOREWORD

In the study of warfare, great men have concluded that there are some overriding principles which, if followed, will always tend toward success in battle, and with equal positiveness, if neglected or ignored, will tend toward defeat or even destruction. These principles have been entitled "the principles of war."

All except the most naive know that the Christian is engaged in a warfare.

All except the most foolish know that in war it is imperative that those involved apply the principles of war.

Just as these time-tried principles are effective in waging secular warfare—the author presents in quick succession these same principles as the key to assured victory in our spiritual warfare.

In the true military style of being brief, perspicuous, and succinct, the author with power plunges the reader point-blank into the fight—a very present institution. The enemy is Satan, the objective is the acknowledgment and fulfillment of the commandments of God, and the ammunition is the power of the Holy Spirit.

The Christian, clothed in the whole armor of God and applying these pertinent guiding principles of warfare—is an army, a communication system, a weapon to be used and a soldier to participate forcibly in the battle, to the glory of our Lord.

Granville A. Sharpe
Colonel, Infantry

PREFACE

> There exists a small number of funda-
> mental principles of war which could not
> be deviated from without danger and the
> application of which on the contrary has
> been in almost all time crowned with
> success.
>
> —*Antoine Henri Jomini*

Every person living today, or just about every
person living today, is conscious of war. He
knows what it is. He has lived through one,
two, or three wars, and if he has not yet lived
with them, he has studied them in school or
he anticipates them in the near future. Everything we do has as either its backdrop or its
future the possibility of war. War is no
stranger to us. Although there is a difference
between physical warfare and spiritual warfare, there is still a close relationship. In fact,
all physical warfare is part of the spiritual
war.

James says in the fourth chapter, "From whence
come wars and fightings among you? Come they
not hence, even of your lusts that war in your
members?" Notice that the physical war and physical fighting come from the lust that is warring
in our members. "Ye lust, and have not; ye kill,

and desire to have, and cannot obtain: ye fight and war, yet ye have not, because ye ask not. Ye ask, and receive not, because ye ask amiss, that ye may consume it upon your lusts."

Physical warfare is a result of being defeated in the spiritual war. However, in this book we are going to be studying mostly the spiritual war having to do with evangelism; and in order to study this we are going to look at the principles of war that have been studied and understood by those generals and tacticians and strategists who are expert at physical war. In the Scriptures there are many parables and metaphors that liken the Christian life to things that we see upon this earth. However, when it comes to warfare, this is not a parable, nor is it a likeness. It's the real thing. In 1 Peter 2:11, Peter writes, "Dearly beloved, I beseech you as strangers and pilgrims, abstain from fleshly lusts, which war against the soul." The Christian life is not likened to a war: it is war, and therefore anything that we can learn to be more effective combatants in this warfare for real victory, both personally and as a body of believers, is of legitimate concern and should be considered primary.

Different experts in warfare list the principles of war numbering from four to fifteen. Those who have a smaller list of principles generally combine different truths under one heading. In this series of studies we are considering eleven principles of war:

1. Objective
2. Offensive

3. Concentration
4. Mobility
5. Security
6. Surprise
7. Cooperation
8. Communication
9. Economy of force
10. Pursuit
11. Obedience

In the following essays it will be my intention to show that these principles of war should be used in the spiritual warfare because first, we are at war; second, they are effective in gaining victory in this war; third, they are biblical; fourth, they are historic principles. The war in which we are engaged is more deadly than the totality of all wars ever fought. This is a war against the soul. Every man is personally engaged in it. He is either a captive and a servant of Satan or a captive and servant of Jesus Christ. Since we are involved in this war, let us take instruction from the experts in physical war and from the Scriptures.

This series of articles originally appeared in ten issues of *Command* magazine, the official organ of the Officers' Christian Fellowship. They were originally written at the insistence and encouragement of Cleo Buxton, Executive Secretary of the Officers' Christian Fellowship and Mr. Robert Coote, editor of *Command*.

The end of each chapter has a portion of Scripture to be studied. The questions are not study questions, with the exception of Chapters 2 and 11; they are on the whole, application questions. They should not be answered until the content of the Scripture portion and the chapter have been studied. Study questions should focus on the content: "What does it say?" Application questions entail: "What am I going to do about what it says?"

I would like to express my appreciation to those who typed the manuscript—Miss Lucy Brouse, Mrs. Don Ross, Mrs. Fred Panetti, and Marny Menkes. Mr. Joseph T. Bayly of David C. Cook Publishing Co. has been a great encouragement to me to publish these articles in book form. Lt. Gen. William K. Harrison, Jr., has gone over the manuscript, checking it for military error or error in principle. Mr. John Wysong, professor of English at the U.S. Naval Academy, has gone over the writing.

ONE
Objective

In war then, let your great object be victory, not lengthy campaigns. —*Sun Tzu, 500* B.C.

But thanks be to God! He gives us the victory through our Lord Jesus Christ.[1]
—*The Apostle Paul.*

When war is declared by Congress their objective[2] is victory. They pass this assignment over to the Commander-in-Chief. The Commander-in-Chief with the Joint Chiefs of Staff makes an estimate of the situation, comes to a decision, and develops a plan. To oversimplify it, the decision might be to invade and occupy specific nations in Europe and Asia. The plan would be to assign Asia to Commander-in-Chief, Pacific; and Europe to Commander-in-Chief, Atlantic. These subordinate commanders must then make an estimate of the situation, come to a decision, and develop a plan. They, in turn, assign objectives to subordinate commanders.

Commander-in-Chief, Pacific, orders the Commander of the Seventh Fleet to land certain armies and Marine Divisions in the assigned country in Asia. This process of estimating the situation, making a decision, and assigning objectives to subordinate commanders continues right down to the company, platoon, and squad level. Every man in the chain of command has his objective assigned to him by higher authority.

Now, suppose an individual infantryman has as his objective the top of a sand dune on a beach in Asia. He is pinned down by enemy fire and he cannot make a move. While he is in this position he suddenly sees a paper floating across the beach.

So far, this is a very realistic situation; but suppose we make it unreal, even ludicrous. The paper happens to be a page from the Joint Chiefs of Staff Operation Order. As the page lands in front of him, he reads the assigned objective to the Commander-in-Chief, Pacific: "Invade and occupy—on the continent of Asia." This is too much for him. He cannot even get off the beach and they are telling him to occupy the whole nation. To him it is unrealistic. Since he cannot understand how the whole can be taken, he might even lose the will to get to the top of the sand dune.

Enough of the illustration. Jesus Christ is our Commander-in-Chief and he has assigned the overall objective and put it in the grasp of every one of his followers in the directive of the Great Commission:

> All power is given unto me in heaven and in earth. Go ye, therefore and teach all nations (Matthew 28:18, 19).

To any individual Christian who thinks he is fighting the war all by himself, this objective seems not only unrealistic, but impossible. Like the soldier on the beach, it is easy to adopt a "What's the use?" attitude.

The problem is the same in both cases. The man at the bottom of the chain gets a view of the objective of the person at the top. He is looking up the chain of command without the benefit of intermediate objectives. He sees only the objective of the top and the resources at the bottom.

So it is for the Christian. He may see with his Commander-in-Chief the complete objective assigned to the whole church. He may also see the smaller parts of the church, groups of believers raised up to reach a special segment of the world's population. God has raised up specialists with limited objectives in his church.

Rather than lament the multiplicity of Christian organizations, we should rejoice that an intensive effort to meet our objective is being made. Of course, there is a danger that such groups will be filled with too great a sense of importance. If, however, they seek to occupy their own limited objective with all faithfulness, then the warfare of the church is advanced. These many organizations may be in existence, not because of doctrinal differences, but because God has given them different objectives under the Great Commission.

The first objective is one of sowing the seed. The second is reaping the harvest when the seed falls on good ground. If we sow the seed in every heart but do not reap where the seed prepares a harvest, then we have not reached our objective. We have in effect added to the condemnation of men with the gospel. We have been a savor of death unto death rather than life unto life (2 Corinthians 2:16).

If, on the other hand, we reap where we have sown but we do not sow in every heart in our assigned mission fields, then we still have not reached our objective. This is serious. This objective is not a mere psychological goal that makes us feel good when we get there. This is a mission assigned by our Commander-in-Chief. Not to get there is failure to carry out the assigned mission: it is defeat. Even if people do not or will not respond to the message of good news, this has no bearing on the objective to communicate the message to them. God assigns the objective; the people do not choose their own.

During the next two generations the number will multiply and turn over several times. The next generation of Christians will be responsible for their generation as we are for ours.

Unless we know where we are going, it is of little importance how we go about getting there. The objective is primary.

QUESTIONS

1. Study personally and/or in a group:
   Matthew 28:16-20 and Colossians 1:24-29.
2. Who assigns our objectives?
3. How can I know what has been assigned
   to me?
4. What are the objectives assigned to us as a
   local body of believers?
5. What are the objectives assigned to my
   family?
6. What are the objectives assigned to me?
7. Is there a time limit given in accomplishing
   the objective?

TWO
Offensive

They want war too methodical, too
measured; I would make it brisk, bold,
impetuous, perhaps sometimes even auda-
cious.
—*Jomini*

This is what is written: "The Christ will
suffer and rise from the dead on the third
day, and repentance and forgiveness of sins
will be preached in his name to all nations,
beginning at Jerusalem."[1]
—*Jesus Christ*

In warfare the offensive is the means by
which one takes the objective. It is an
aggressive advance against an enemy to wrest
the objective from his possession.

An army on the offensive has a moral and
physical advantage over the enemy at the
point of contact. The offensive is an attitude
as well as an action. The attacking general
has the advantage of making his decisions
first, and then carrying them out. The
defender must first wait to see what his
opponent does before he makes his decision.
The decision he makes is usually forced upon
him by the attacker. The aggressor has the
advantage of the initiative. He can choose
whether to attack and when and where to

attack. The defender must wait for him. He is in the superior position.

There are two general ways in which the offensive can be directed.

1. It may be directed against the whole front to take the whole front simultaneously. This is not ordinarily feasible in that it requires an overwhelming superiority in numbers and weapons. Nor is it wise, for it requires much more logistic (weapons, food, ammunition) support, much more fighting, and will sustain many more casualties.

2. The offensive may be directed against one segment of the enemy army, the defeat of which will mean a decisive victory. "Decisive" means that this defeat of the enemy may cause the rest of the army to capitulate, or it may mean a breakthrough has been made so that the rest of the army remains in a very weak position.

"In either case it should be well understood that there is in every battlefield a decisive point, the possession of which, more than any other, helps to secure the victory by enabling its holder to make proper application of the Principles of War. Arrangements should therefore be made for striking the Decisive blow upon this point" (Jomini).

There are two things which determine a "decisive point." The first is the relative importance of that point compared to the rest of the front. The second is the feasibility of taking that point. If it is not important, it is not decisive. If it is important but not feasible to take, then it is not decisive. This is very important. Be alert for teaching on the decisive point in succeeding chapters.

Whether the offense is made along the whole front or at a decisive point, it has several basic characteristics. In attitude it is bold; in direction it is forward toward the enemy at the objective; as its means it uses effective weapons.

The offensive in the spiritual war is conducted in the same manner. It is directed against the enemy, not against the objective. Satan is the enemy. We fight in order to wrest from his possession those who through fear of death are subject to his bondage.[2]

Most of this spiritual war is already history. Jesus Christ delivered the decisive blow at the decisive point at the decisive time. The blow was his death for sin and sinners. The point was a cross outside the city of Jerusalem and the time was the feast of the Passover about A.D. 30. The Bible tells us that this blow destroyed the enemy and set the prisoners free. When Jesus died on the cross he cried with a loud voice, "It is finished." What was finished? The defeat and ultimate destruction of Satan! This was the emancipation proclamation which sets us free from Satan. "If the Son therefore shall make you free, ye shall be free indeed."[3]

What remains if the decisive blow has been struck? We must occupy the land. We must proclaim the emancipation to Satan's captives. We must declare the means of freedom, the gospel, the defeat of Satan, and the victory of Christ in his death and resurrection. We participate in that ancient victory, for its proclamation is still unfinished. It is still news which many captives have not heard.

The offensive in the spiritual war is to be carried out by two very basic means: preaching and prayer. Preaching, when done in the power of the Holy Spirit, is an engagement on the spiritual plane. Other powers are in conflict besides the speaker and the listeners. In 2 Timothy 2 we can see *four* participants in the conflict: the Lord's servant, the opponent, God, and the devil.

> Have nothing to do with stupid, senseless controversies; you know that they breed quarrels. And the Lord's servant must not be quarrelsome but kindly to every one, an apt teacher, forbearing, correcting his opponents with gentleness. God may perhaps grant that they will repent and come to know the truth, and they may escape from the snare of the devil, after being captured by him to do his will (2 Timothy 2:23-26, RSV).

When the Christian teaches in the power of the Holy Spirit, he does it without quarreling. The strife is on the spiritual plane. He teaches with gentleness.

The offensive in preaching is commanded in many places in the New Testament. One of the more dynamic expressions is the word of the angel who opened the prison doors in Acts 5:20 and said, "Go and stand in the temple and speak to the people all the words of this life."

Praying in the Holy Spirit is also commanded in the New Testament. Two of these examples are:

21

First of all, then, I urge that supplications, prayers, intercessions, and thanksgivings be made for all men, for kings and all who are in high positions, that we may lead a quiet and peaceable life, godly and respectful in every way. This is good, and it is acceptable in the sight of God our Savior, who desires all men to be saved and to come to the knowledge of the truth. For there is one God, and there is one mediator between God and men, the man Christ Jesus, who gave himself as a ransom for all, the testimony to which was borne at the proper time (1 Timothy 2:1-6, RSV).

Pray at all times in the Spirit, with all prayer and supplication. To that end keep alert with all perseverance, making supplication for all the saints, and also for me, that utterance may be given me in opening my mouth boldly to proclaim the mystery of the gospel, for which I am an ambassador in chains; that I may declare it boldly, as I ought to speak (Ephesians 6:18-20, RSV).

Notice this. The first text says "First of all," and the last is the concluding thought of the paragraph that starts "Finally" (v. 10). "First" and "finally," that is the order of prayer. Then notice that both of these paragraphs on prayer have to do with evangelism. When we pray in the Spirit, we and others will preach in the Spirit boldly. Ephesians 6:10-20 is very clear teaching on spiritual warfare and prayer is the final part of it. What Paul teaches in these three verses he practices in the earlier chapters where his own prayers are recorded in Ephesians 1:16-21 and 3:14-19.

These prayers are for Christians. His prayer requests are also for Christians. We have few passages in the New Testament on prayer for unbelievers; four that I have found are: Jesus' prayer on the cross (Luke 23:34), Stephen's dying prayer (Acts 7:60), Paul's prayer for his countrymen ("Brethren, my heart's desire and prayer to God for them is that they may be saved," Romans 10:1, RSV), and the 1 Timothy passage quoted earlier. All of them are evangelistic prayers. The prayers for Christians and prayer requests for Christians are more numerous and they also have to do with the proclamation of the gospel, as in Ephesians 6:20: "that I may declare it boldly, as I ought to speak."

Jesus, in Matthew 9, when he saw the multitudes and had compassion on them, commanded:

> The harvest is plentiful, but the laborers are few; pray therefore the Lord of the harvest to send out laborers into his harvest (Matthew 9:37, 38, RSV).

Again, it is evangelism. We take the offensive under orders, praying and preaching in the Holy Spirit. Our objective is people: individuals, cities, and nations. The enemy holds them captive at his own will. Then let us move out; let us advance toward the objective, praying and preaching.

QUESTIONS

1. Who is the Enemy? Name him.
2. Who is the objective? Name him or them.
3. How should we pray for unbelievers?
4. How should we pray for believers?
   Study: Colossians 1:9-14; Philippians 1:9-11; Ephesians 6:18-20; Ephesians 3:14-19; 1:15-23; and Colossians 4:2-4. Look carefully at every phrase in the texts. What do the texts say about power? What do they say about wisdom? What do they say about speaking the gospel? What else do they say?
5. Make an agreement with each other to pray for one another with the content found in these biblical prayers and prayer requests.
6. Name other believers for whom you will pray.
7. Continue the discussion on preaching, using 1 Thessalonians 1:4—2:9. Go into this text in detail, noticing every positive characteristic about the proclamation of the gospel. Also list the ways the gospel is *not* to be preached.
8. Is there a "decisive point" in your city or state where you can concentrate prayer and witness?

THREE
Concentration

I git thar fustest with the mostest.
—*Gen. Nathan Bedford Forrest,*
               War Between the States

For where two or three come together in my
name, there am I with them.[1]   —*Jesus Christ*

General Forrest was neither a West Pointer
nor a War College graduate, but he knew the
principles of war and he knew how to apply
them. Although it is doubtful that he used the
double superlatives in the above quotation,
the statement does emphasize several truths.
In this one short sentence we find four[2]
principles of war, and others are implied. The
one word "mostest" leads us to the subject of
this "Concentration."

Neither Alexander the Great nor Julius
Caesar could have conquered the then known
world if he had neglected concentration.

Occasionally in the history of warfare a new
method comes to light that seems so effective
or is such a surprise to the enemy that its
users are strongly tempted to depend upon the
new method (which is temporary) and forget
the principles of war, such as concentration.

This tendency was evident when the
airplane made its advent on the Western

Front in World War I. It glamorized the war; men became air aces and heroes. The use of the airplane did not, however, have much effect on the final outcome, for no one used it in concentration.

Major General Claire Chennault, when a young Army Air Corps aviator, noted this lack of application of principle. In his *Way of a Fighter,* he wrote:

> For four months we flew and fought all over the Texas sky in the fashion of the Western Front—flying long patrols in formation, looking for a fight, and then scattering in a dive on the enemy into individual dogfights. As sport it was superb, but as war, even then, it seemed all wrong to me. There was too much of an air of medieval jousting in the dogfights and not enough of the calculated massing of overwhelming force so necessary in the cold, cruel business of war. There were no sound military precepts that encouraged the dispersion of forces and firepower that occurred in dogfighting (*Way of a Fighter,* G. P. Putnam's Sons, New York; p. 11).

This failure to apply the principle of concentration continued through the Spanish Civil War and into World War II. Chennault himself put an end to these individual tactics with his American Volunteer Group, better known as the Flying Tigers. When he went to Burma and China, his pilots stuck together. Outnumbered in the air and on the ground, in planes, pilots, and parts, they destroyed 217 enemy planes and probably 43 more with a maximum of 20 operational P-40's in 31 encounters. Chennault's losses were six pilots and sixteen planes. In order to accomplish this, Chennault used concentration. He simply had two aircraft firing at one enemy aircraft. Even if outnumbered in the air ten to one, Chennault's two always outnumbered the enemy's one. If each Flying Tiger had taken on ten of the enemy, probably we would not remember the Flying Tigers today.

In 1956 while on the staff of Commander Carrier Division Five aboard the aircraft carrier *Shangri-la* in the western Pacific, I watched the Carrier Air Group in practice maneuvers. The F9F Cougars came down from the sky low over the waves, firing machine guns or rockets at the target simultaneously, then pulled up together to disappear into the blue. One evening I asked one of the pilots how he could fly wing on his leader and still aim at the target. It was easy, he said; he did not aim, he just flew wing. "When he shoots, I shoot." This is concentration.

Now let us see how the principle of concentration applies to spiritual warfare.

After these things the Lord appointed other seventy also, and sent them two and two before his face into every city and place, whither he himself would come. Therefore said he unto them, The harvest truly is great, but the labourers are few: pray ye therefore the Lord of the harvest, that he would send forth labourers into his harvest (Luke 10:1, 2).

In the chapter on "The Offensive" we concluded that the offense in winning men to Jesus Christ is carried out by preaching and prayer. In the Luke passage we see that Jesus sent his disciples out to preach in concentration. He also told them to pray in concentration: "Again I say unto you, that if two of you shall agree on earth as touching any thing that they shall ask, it shall be done for them of my Father which is in heaven. For where two or three are gathered together in my name there am I in the midst of them" (Matthew 18:19, 20). This is effective warfare.

Paul, one of the greatest of preachers, had a "wing man" with him in most cases, and when alone he does not seem to have been nearly as effective. For instance, in Acts 17 we find Paul going to Athens alone but asking that Silas and Timothy join him with "all speed." "Now while Paul waited for them at Athens, his spirit was stirred in him, when he saw the city wholly given to idolatry. Therefore disputed he in the synagogue with the Jews, and with the devout persons, and in the market daily." Paul could not wait to concentrate his forces; so he took the city on alone and had neither an awakening nor a riot. Silas and Timothy did not join him until some weeks after Paul had arrived in Corinth. Here also he preached alone with no recorded results.

> And he reasoned in the synagogue every sabbath, and persuaded the Jews and the Greeks (Acts 18:4).

When Silas and Timothy arrived, there was a marked difference in the power, the content, and the results of Paul's preaching.

> And when Silas and Timotheus were come from Macedonia, Paul was *pressed in the spirit*, and testified to the Jews that Jesus was Christ (Acts 18:5).

That was the power and the content; the results are recorded in succeeding sentences. There was opposition, blasphemy, and many conversions.

> And Crispus, the chief ruler of the synagogue, believed on the Lord with all his house; and many of the Corinthians hearing believed, and were baptized.
> Then spake the Lord to Paul in the night by a vision, Be not afraid, but speak, and hold not thy peace: For I am with thee, and no man shall set on thee to hurt thee: for I have *much* people in this city (Acts 18:8-10).

Paul remained in Corinth among these many believers for another eighteen months teaching the Word of God among them.

Concentration was so important to Paul that he wrote on one occasion:

> When I came to Troas to preach Christ's gospel, and a door was opened unto me of the Lord, I had no rest in my spirit, because I found not Titus my brother: but taking my

leave of them, I went from thence into
Macedonia (2 Corinthians 2:12, 13).

Paul passed by an open door for lack of help.

Many of us wish we had an Apostle Paul to
travel with, not realizing how much the leader
also needs the close follower. Without his
helpers, Paul was not greatly used in Athens or
Troas. When the earthquake occurred at
midnight in Philippi, it was not Paul alone who
prayed, but Paul and Silas. There are many
other instances in the Bible where concentration proved important to the gospel ministry.

If you find that you are scattering your
witness in "dogfights" or if the enemy is using
concentration on you because you insist on
taking the whole ship or base or city alone,
then you need a partner. You may be partly
effective in your lone witness and you may
think you have no need for a wing man.
Perhaps you do not, but maybe the wing man
needs a leader. Remember that in warfare it is
not enough to be faithful but only partly
effective. We are after the objective.

You may wonder where you are going to find
a partner. Start by asking God to send him or
her along. You may have to lead the person to
the Lord. Once you meet him and before you
minister together, you need to be one in
purpose and as complementary as possible.
Study together, pray together, talk together, and
reprove one another in the Lord. There should
be openness and honesty between the two and
no unconfessed sin to hide. Then you can meet

the enemy with combined fire power.

A few years ago aboard a carrier in the Pacific, two junior officers met every afternoon to offer concentrated prayer for the ship. Soon one other officer received Christ; this increased the concentration 50 percent. In two months ten officers and over thirty enlisted men were reached for Christ through this concentrated prayer and witness. The witness continued.

Concentration also plays a vital part in mass evangelism. In the chapter "Offensive" it was brought out that when the army on the offense does not possess an overwhelming superiority it is not feasible to launch an attack along the whole front to take the objective. In such a case a decisive point must be selected against which to strike a decisive blow. An overwhelming superiority must be gained at the chosen point. This superiority is obtained by transferring forces from the rest of the line to the decisive point. This weakens the rest of the line, but enough should be left in order to keep the enemy occupied. Even if minor defeats occur along the weakened portion, this is not crucial, because in the meantime you have served the decisive blow at the decisive point which defeats the enemy.

An excellent example of this is found in Montgomery's preparations for the first battle of El Alamein. In his own words:

> Then from the bits and pieces in Egypt I was going to form a new corps, the 10th Corps, strong in armour; this would never

hold the line but would be to us what the Afrika Korps was to Rommel; the formation of this new 10th Corps had already begun.

Montgomery concluded that Rommel would make his main effort on the south or inland flank. This was the Alam Halfa Ridge. Since Montgomery weakened his northern flank in order to concentrate on Alam Halfa, he strengthened it with mine fields and wire so it could be held with a minimum of troops. At Alam Halfa, the decisive point, he concentrated two mobile armored divisions, the 44th Infantry Division, and his newly formed armored division of 400 tanks dug in behind a screen of six-pounder anti-tank guns. From August 31 to September 6, 1942, the Afrika Korps pounded against this line, all the while being hit hard by the mobile and dug-in tanks and by the British Desert Air Force. Rommel retreated on the 6th with a decimated Afrika Korps. He had been defeated and Montgomery had won a decisive victory. Thus, concentration achieved the turning point of the war in Africa.

Non-Christians and the powers of darkness outnumber us along the whole front in the spiritual warfare. We can make advances along this front by using two-by-two concentration. This is necessary; however, it may not bring a decisive victory. In order to win a decisive victory we must seek the will of God to determine the decisive points. Then Christians along the whole front will:

    1. Concentrate on prayer for the decisive points.

2. Transfer temporarily or permanently to the decisive point for concentrated preaching and testifying.

The physical transfer could be made by taking time off and traveling to the decisive point. This would weaken portions of the front temporarily, but no more so than when Christians take leave under ordinary circumstances.

When Jesus gave the Great Commission the apostles were not sent immediately to the uttermost parts of the earth. They were told to remain together in Jerusalem until they were "endued with power from on high" (Luke 24:49). Notice the elements of concentration:

1. They were all together.
2. They all continued together in prayer.
3. They were all in agreement.
4. They all preached the wonderful works of God (Acts 2:11).

As a result of concentrated prayer and preaching, 3,000 were won to Christ in one day.

The same sort of concentration is practiced in the Billy Graham campaigns. Thousands of Christian people pray for him, the team, and the city for weeks and months in advance of the crusade. Hundreds more concentrate in the city as counselors, choir members, and assistant missioners weeks in advance and during the crusade.

Pray ye therefore the Lord of the harvest, that he would send forth labourers into his harvest (Luke 10:2).

QUESTIONS
1. Study Acts 16:11-40.
2. Do you have a partner with whom you can pray? Who is he?
3. Do you have a partner with whom you can witness? Who is he?
4. What can you do to be involved in a larger group in prayer?
5. What can you do to be involved in a larger group in proclaiming the gospel?

FOUR
Mobility

And thus shall ye eat it; with your loins
girded, your shoes on your feet, and your
staff in your hand; and ye shall eat it in
haste: it is the Lord's passover.

—Exodus 12:11

But God's word is not chained.[1]

—*the Apostle Paul*

After 400 years, some of which had been
spent in slavery, 600,000 men of Israel,
besides women, children, and possessions,
moved out of the land of Egypt in one night.
That is mobility! If we undertook the same
feat today we would use trains, planes, trucks,
and ships. We would have better equipment
but might not prove as mobile.

Mobility as a principle of war is not
absolute. It must not be measured against how
fast we could move yesterday; rather it must
be compared with the enemy's mobility. We
must move more quickly, farther, and for a
greater period of time than the enemy.
Mobility was defined in the statement of
General Nathan Bedford Forrest, "I git thar
fustest with the mostest."

The French of World War II could move
their armies but they were not as mobile as

35

the armies of Hitler. Hitler's Lightning Warfare (Blitzkrieg) was mobility in action. The early successes of the Japanese in the same war were largely dependent upon the mobility of their striking and invasion forces. The political and military surprises of both Germany and Japan could not have been effected without military mobility.

The opposite of mobility is immobility. To be immobilized is to be at the mercy of the enemy. An army or any other unit that is immobilized is incapable of attacking, evading, or retreating. It can only defend until surrender or to the end. The American defense of Corregidor is an example of immobility.

The British Army was defeated in France in 1940. If it had reached the coast and found that it was immobilized it would not have suffered defeat only; it would have been annihilated. It was the British mobility at sea which saved the Army at Dunkirk. If the Germans had been as mobile at sea as they were on land, they could have followed the British across the Channel. In this case the defenders were mobile and the victors became immobile.

In Word War II mobility was demonstrated in the existence and actions of the U.S. Third and Fifth Fleets. One component of the Third-Fifth Fleet[2] particularly exemplified mobility. This was the Fast Carrier Striking Force, Task Force 38 (or 58, under the Fifth Fleet) under the command of Vice Admiral Marc Mitscher. This force could move hundreds of miles overnight in any direction and strike hundreds of miles farther with the Air Groups. It consisted of fifteen or sixteen carriers and scores of screening ships.

The nuclear submarine and the Strategic Air Command are probably the most mobile of present-day combat units. In the infantry the Army's Airborne Divisions and the FMF of the Marine Corps are probably the most mobile. One of their characteristics is their ability to strike a decisive blow any place of their own choosing. The offense could never be mounted in concentration without the ability to move. An army must be mobile.

Jesus Christ said, "Go ye into all the world, and preach the gospel to every creature" (Mark 16:15).

From the above command and other texts in the New Testament we, in previous chapters, drew the conclusion that "every creature" is the objective and that preaching and prayer were our two main means of offense. From the same text we see that mobility is a requirement if we are to carry out Christ's command to "Go."

Within the church there must be an ability to move to the place or to the people where the offense will take place. We must convey our firepower where it will be used. Securing this mobility is simply a matter of obedience to the command "Go."

We can move our firepower in many of the ways that physical weapons of war are moved. We can walk. Philip left Samaria and was, in obedience to God, crossing the desert when he encountered the Ethiopian eunuch. Philip taught Christ to him from Isaiah 53 and the man believed. David Brainerd moved on horseback and led hundreds of American Indians to Jesus Christ. In Jungle Camp the Wycliffe Bible Translators are trained to move by foot, raft, and dugout canoe. The Missionary Aviation Fellowship provides mobility superior to that of the enemy in territory which is otherwise inaccessible.

There are other ways of delivering the Word of God besides taking the messenger to the physical location. One is that of correspondence. God put his stamp of approval on this means of mobility when much of the New Testament was given to us in letters, this being necessitated in part because the messengers, Paul and John, were immobilized as prisoners. Praise God, his Word is not bound.[3]

Another important means is the mobility gained through Christian books and literature sent via mail or passed from hand to hand. The ministry of moving Christian books, magazines, booklets, and Bibles is hardly being used at all. The Christian may be physically immobilized because of his profession or state of health. Yet if he used Christian literature he would not find the Word of God limited just because he himself was immobilized. The objective would be taken in near or distant places, though the Christian was absent.

The giving and sending of books is just the beginning of fast mobile communication of the gospel. Records and tape recordings can bring to anyone's living room the most powerful preaching and teaching that is available today. Christian leaders are broadcasting the gospel of Jesus Christ on hundreds of radio stations weekly. But this does not guarantee that people will have radio receivers tuned on at the time or to the right station. A telephone call to each of our friends immediately before the program would greatly increase the listening audience.

Then too, we should consider mobility with the use of the weapon itself. If a weapon has a 360° field and the soldier keeps it trained in one direction only, then he is not using the weapon's inherent mobility.

Our weapon, the Word of God, " . . . is living and active, sharper than any two-edged sword, piercing to the division of soul and spirit, of joints and marrow, and discerning the thoughts and intentions of the heart" (Hebrews 4:12, RSV). We must use it to the maximum of our capability. It has no limitations. The limitations are in us. Let us learn to use the Word as a defensive-offensive weapon. It is a tragedy to see Christians immobilized in a specific witnessing situation because they do not know how to use a very powerful and effective weapon. If we are versatile in the Scriptures, we can strike an effective blow at the place of our choosing. Continual personal study of the Bible is the only adequate preparation for use of the Word.

All of this so far has had to do with the mobility of our firepower, or, in other words, our witnessing. But from the chapter on the offense we recall that our offense is directed with prayer in addition to preaching. We must be mobile here, also.

Like the Word of God, prayer has no limitations. The limitations are in us. Prayer of intercession has greater range, accuracy, speed, and power than the greatest intercontinental ballistic missile we will ever produce. The prayer of intercession is one that agrees with God in his desire and purpose to win men to himself. We can use as our guide the prayers of Jesus and of the apostles, both for Christian brethren and for those who are still under the command of the enemy.

Jeremiah 33:3 says, "Call unto me, and I will answer thee, and shew thee great and mighty things, which thou knowest not." Let us ask for big things, things which we have never previously experienced.

Mobility serves no purpose if we have no intention of going anywhere. Do not stay at home in your intercession. Be mobile. It costs nothing to go to Africa via God's throne in prayer, except time and a concern for men in Africa.

Dawson Trotman recounts a personal experience in the booklet *Born to Reproduce*. He and a fellow worker in the Navigators, when that organization was still very young, decided to pray for the development of their work in every state of the union:

So we made a list of forty-eight states, and we prayed. Morning after morning in these little prayer meetings we would look at our list and ask God to use us and other young fellows in Washington, in Oregon, in California, and in all other states of the Union. Five weeks went by, and we did not miss a morning. We met at four o'clock on Sunday morning and spent three hours in prayer. During the sixth week the Lord put it on our hearts to get a map of the world, and we took it up to our little cave in the hill. We began to put our fingers on Germany, France and Italy. We put them on Turkey and Greece. I remember looking at one little island near China—you had to look closely to see what it was—and we prayed that God would use us in the lives of the men in Formosa.

If you know of the worldwide ministry of the Navigators today, you know that this prayer has been answered.

The united witness of which we are a part is also the result of the prayers of many Christians. Let us not stop now; let us individually and together pray to take the objective for Jesus Christ. Pray that we will be used in the lives of others.

The effectiveness of our ministry in the spiritual war largely depends upon the individual mobility in the use of our capabilities: the Word and prayer. We must know something of the range and depth of the Word of God and we must experience the range and accuracy of intercessory prayer.

And it shall come to pass, that before they call, I will answer; and while they are yet speaking, I will hear (Isaiah 65:24).

QUESTIONS
1. Study 1 Timothy 2:1-7.
2. Are you immobilized in your witness because of your lack of knowledge of the Bible?

3. Are you immobilized because of not praying?
4. Think of ways that you as an individual can and will increase your mobility with the gospel.
5. How will you implement these new ways?

FIVE
Security

The art of retrenchment . . . shall serve
the defender NOT to defend himself more
securely behind a rampart, but to attack
the enemy more successfully. —*Clausewitz*

Finally, my brethren, be strong in the
Lord, and in the power of his might. Put on
the whole armour of God, that ye may be
able to stand against the wiles of the devil.
For we wrestle not against flesh and blood,
but against principalities, against powers,
against the rulers of the darkness of this
world, against spiritual wickedness in high
places. Wherefore take unto you the whole
armour of God, that ye may be able to
withstand in the evil day, and having done
all, to stand.[1]   —*the Apostle Paul*

The subject of security may be divided into three
parts:
1. Intelligence of the enemy;
2. Continual protection against the enemy;
3. Final stand against the enemy.

Before we can be secure from attacks by an
enemy we must know there is an enemy. The
nation that has no enemy is very secure. The
nation that has an enemy but does not think

so is very insecure. That nation could be surprised, completely unprotected.

Intelligence of an enemy insures knowing who he is, his intentions, and his methods of operating. This prevents deception and surprise. In physical warfare this intelligence is gained by listening to everything the enemy says and reading everything he writes. Since the enemy does not want his opponent listening in on everything he says, he establishes safeguards: fences, guards, sound-proof rooms, security checks to expose spies or traitors, and encryption of his radio and telephone communications. In order to gain this intelligence the opponent sends in spies, breaks down fences, steals safes, bribes or kills guards, taps telephone wires, and practices cryptanalysis.

Thus, to be secure from the enemy, one must gain access to his communications while safeguarding all of his own communications.

In the early months after Pearl Harbor, our carriers were operating in the Southwest Pacific, our battleships were out of action, and the Japanese were moving a three-pronged striking and invasion fleet toward Midway Islands and the Aleutian Chain. There would have been no stopping this force if it had not been for intelligence of the enemy. Through cryptanalysis, the U.S. Navy cracked the Japanese code and moved more planes and submarines to Midway. The Japanese lost four carriers to air action while we lost one carrier and one destroyer. This, the turning point of the war in the Pacific, illustrates the absolute necessity of intelligence of the enemy to insure security.

So it is in spiritual war. Our enemy is Satan. We must know who he is, what he does, his intentions and methods. We can read his history in the Bible and observe his victories and his defeats in his action with men. We can also read of his contact with the Son of God, his failure in the Temptation in the Wilderness and his defeat at Calvary.

We find that Satan is neither omnipotent nor omniscient and that he has very definite limitations. Apparently through ignorance of God's "plan of attack," Satan perpetrated the crucifixion of the Lord Jesus Christ by blinding the religious and political leaders of 2,000 years ago. The Bible says: " . . . none of the princes of this world knew [the wisdom of God]: for had they known it, they would not have crucified the Lord of glory" (1 Corinthians 2:7, 8). This failure of Satan to discern God's plan was a factor in his defeat, for through the cross God wrests men from Satan's grasp and enlists them into his eternal kingdom.

Neither are we omnipotent and omniscient, but we have access to power and knowledge of which Satan knows nothing. Christ has revealed to us the wisdom of God, though it is "hidden" from the world. He also endows us with his power. Christ said to the apostles: "All power is given unto me. Therefore go."

There are many things Satan does not know and cannot do. Let us find out his strength and weakness factors, "Lest," as Paul says in 2 Corinthians 2:11, "Satan should get an advantage of us: for we are not ignorant of his devices." Let us discover the information which is the key to our spiritual security.

Intelligence of Satan permits us to set up our defenses. Ephesians 6:10-17 describes this defense, with the reasons for each part of our "armor." Before we put on the armor we must be strong in the Lord's strength and power (v. 10). Verses 11 to 13 put the emphasis upon the whole of the armor and 14 to 18 speak of the separate parts of the armor and their uses.

Our combatants are not flesh and blood but "principalities," "powers," "rulers of the darkness of this world," "spiritual wickedness in high places" (v. 12), and they are masterminded by the devil himself (v. 11). Like any wise general, Satan will not attack a strong point if weak points are available for a breakthrough. He is a good strategist. We need not fear his strength so much as his "wiles" (v. 11). The Scripture tells us twice to put on the "whole armor of God" so there will be no weak points.

A wall around a city may be strictly defensive, but armor by definition is not. Webster's Collegiate Dictionary says of armor: "that conceived of as an offensive or defensive weapon." A soldier does not cover himself with armor because he intends to read a good book in front of his fireplace. He is going off to battle. He has every intention of going into harm's way. He is looking for and expecting a fight. Sun Tzu said:

> The good fighters of old first put themselves beyond the possibility of defeat and then waited for an opportunity of defeating the enemy.

46

The Christian warrior who obeys Ephesians 6 has done just this. This soldier employs the various parts of the armor to put himself beyond the possibility of defeat. He surrounds himself with truth, he puts on the breastplate of righteousness, he takes the shield of faith and dons his helmet of salvation. Then with the power of the Lord, the preparation of the gospel of peace, and the sword of the Spirit, he defeats the enemy.

If the great objective assigned to us by Jesus Christ is to "preach the gospel to every creature," then the smallest whole number of that objective is one single person. Each individual, like the rest of his fellows, is an enemy of God in his mind by wicked works (Colossians 1:21). We are surrounded by these enemies. We read their literature, hear their conversation, and participate in their community. In effect, the prince of this world and his servants are taking the offensive against the saints continually. One way to keep from being attacked would be to keep no company with the wicked. But 1 Corinthians 5:10 tells us that "then must ye needs go out of the world." Jesus prayed to the Father, "not that thou shouldest take them out of the world, but that thou shouldest keep them from the evil" (John 17:15). It is his will that we be exposed to attack but not defeated. Our divinely ordered armor provides effective security.

Lt. General William K. Harrison, Jr., in a message given in Yokosuka, Japan, drew attention to Romans 13:12-14, which says, "let us put on the armour of light," and "put ye on the Lord Jesus Christ, and make not provision for the flesh, to fulfil the lusts thereof." This indicates, General Harrison said, that *putting on* the armor of Ephesians 6 we are putting on Jesus Christ. He is the truth (John 14:6). He is our righteousness (1 Corinthians 1:30). He is the author and finisher of our faith (Hebrews 12:2). He is the gospel (Mark 1:1). He is our salvation (Exodus 15:2), and he is the Word (John 1:1).

In physical war, if a nation were continually under attack and on the defensive we could prophesy ultimate defeat, surrender, or destruction. To prevent this there must be a final stand. The initiative and the offensive must change hands before victory could come to the defenders. This stand is called the defensive-offensive.

In World War II there were four main turning points which gave the offensive to the Allies. All of these were great defensive-offensive battles where the defenders won and afterward took the initiative. Two of them have already been described in brief. The first battle of Alamein at the Alam Halfa ridge turned the tide in North Africa. It is briefly described in Chapter Three, "Concentration." The Battle of Midway mentioned earlier was the defensive-offensive battle that reversed the positions in the Central Pacific. In Europe the crown for defensive-offensive strategy goes to the Russians in the Battle of Stalingrad. When it became clear that the city would not fall, the Germans should have called a retreat. This was not done and the German Sixth Army was annihilated. The fourth example is the defense of Port Moresby in New Guinea which resulted in the annihilation of the Japanese Detachment at Buna.

If there is no turning point, the defender will be defeated. There will be no turning unless a stand is made in a defensive-offensive battle. Yet, seemingly, in the minds of many Christians, a defensive position in the spiritual life is considered a virtue and an offensive position a sin. Defense is associated with the innocent party, as though we expect only the wicked to take up the offense. For this reason the virtuous pride themselves on being defenders, instead of taking up the offensive for truth, justice, holiness, and a powerful personal witness. This sometimes results in the pathetic situation of the virtuous enjoying defeat. Let us never forget that without an eventual offensive, defense only anticipates ultimate defeat.

The defensive-offensive applies to both individuals and groups of believers. Have you been only a defender against sin and sinners? Perhaps it is time for a stand, a defensive-offensive.

"Therefore stand," and thus make your security sure.

QUESTIONS
1. Study Ephesians 6:10-20.
2. Do you have the power of God?
3. Do you have the complete armor?
4. Are you willing to make a stand at work on moral and ethical issues?
5. Are you willing to make a stand for Jesus Christ at work?

SIX
Surprise

One belligerent must surprise, the other
must be surprised. Only and when the two
Commanders play these respective roles
will a battle lead to the annihilation of one
Army.   —*General Waldemar Erfurth*

And they were filled with wonder and amazement at what had happened to him.
                                        —Acts 3:10, NIV

The Old Testament hero Gideon learned
the principles of war by revelation from God,
and one of them was "surprise." The account
in Judges tells us that the amassed armies of
the "Midianites and the Amalekites and all
the children of the east lay along in the valley
like grasshoppers." This force consisted of
135,000. Less than 15,000 got away. We can
say that Gideon with 300 men surprised the
enemy and won a battle of annihilation.

There are only a few elements with which
surprise can be effected: time, place, and
method, or any combination of the three.

However, surprise also depends upon two
additional and essential factors, namely,
ignorance on the part of one commander, and
intelligence on the part of the other. This
ignorance may be natural (e.g., incompetence

or inadequate security) or it may be induced (deception).

Gideon's victory, Hannibal's victory at Cannae, the German invasion through the Ardennes in 1940, and the Japanese attack on Pearl Harbor were all aided by the ignorance of the surprised nation. In the first two cases deception helped immensely in the execution of the surprise, and in all four cases the surprising belligerent kept his intentions and plans secret.

The surprise of Gideon was one of time (night) and method (lamps, torches, voices, trumpets) and place (three sides of the camp). The attack on Pearl Harbor was a surprise of time and place; the weapon was not unusual. The United States' surprise at Hiroshima and Nagasaki was primarily one of weapon, although the time and place were a part of the surprise.

In the spiritual warfare we may use any or all of these elements of surprise. Surprise can be very effectively used in evangelism, whether mass evangelism (strategic surprise) or in personal evangelism (tactical surprise).

In the spiritual war there are two commanders, God and the devil. One of them is the Creator, the other a created being. God is omniscient, Satan is not. Since surprise depends upon the ignorance (natural or induced) of one of the commanders, it becomes obvious that God cannot be surprised. God is omniscient. He has no limitations in his intelligence, nor can he be deceived.

This is not true of the devil. He has been

surprised before. God did not deceive Satan. He just withheld information from him. The Bible speaks of it over and over as a mystery (cf. 1 Corinthians 2:7, 8).

> For when we were yet without strength, in due time Christ died for the ungodly. For scarcely for a righteous man will one die: yet peradventure for a good man some would even dare to die. But God commendeth his love toward us, in that, while we were yet sinners, Christ died for us (Romans 5:6-8).

Surprise in warfare means more than "to cause wonder or astonishment or amazement because of something unexpected." It means "to attack or capture suddenly and without warning." The above passage from Romans 5 clearly tells us that the love of Christ expressed in his death for us is unexpected. If the message is used with people who are dependent on their own effort or relative goodness, they will be "amazed." If the messenger catches that man with his defense down, he will be "amazed" and surprised. In other words, he will be captured suddenly and without warning.

Surprise may be increased even more if we combine the message with a surprise in time and place. To hear the gospel in a Sunday evening evangelistic church service is no surprise. It is even possible that the message itself will surprise no one in the audience. On the other hand, a personal testimony of the saving grace of Jesus Christ backed up with the Word of God will be an effective surprise when it comes from a line officer. It will surprise tellingly when this occurs in a bar, at a cocktail party, in the office, in the field, aboard ship, or in combat.

It is much easier to be vocal in an evangelical church than it is in the above places. It is always easier to train for combat than it is to engage the enemy in a fire fight. The reason is simple: in the evangelical church, as in military training, there is no enemy. The presence of an enemy means fear and knots in the stomach, even though we have the opportunity to take the initiative and catch him by surprise.

On the defensive we have no choice but to fight. But when we have the opportunity to surprise the enemy, the decision to fight is ours. We would hardly pass up such an opportunity in physical combat, though it means fear and the possibility of death. Likewise let us press our advantages in spiritual warfare, despite the problems and fears. Do not reject surprise in time and place.

To forewarn the enemy is to ask for strong resistance to any attack. The principle of surprise is one of the prime means of thwarting such resistance. This principle applies equally in personal evangelism. If we give men the chance, they will hide, cover up, and defend sin. They will do the same with their ignorance. They will make a last stand defending sin even if it is only bluff. Let us catch men with their guards down. Give them as little opportunity as possible to hide or defend sin.

Above all, use the Word of God: "For the

53

word of God is living and active, sharper than any two-edged sword, piercing to the division of soul and spirit, of joints and marrow, and discerning the thoughts and intentions of the heart. And before him no creature is hidden, but all are open and laid bare to the eyes of him with whom we have to do" (Hebrews 4:12, 13, RSV). This is our surprise. It is devastating. Remember our objective is not to win an argument, but to win men to Jesus Christ.

QUESTIONS
1. Study the temptations of Eve (Genesis 3:1-6) and Jesus (Matthew 4:1-11), and also study 1 John 2:15-17.
2. Are you ignorant of Satan's devices?
3. Have you ever been caught by surprise by the Enemy?
4. Can you think of ways that will catch the Enemy by surprise in witnessing?

SEVEN
Cooperation

Fellowship is the keynote of this belief; such a deep fellowship with God through Christ as shall inevitably lead to a deep fellowship with others of His children. The revival of the Christian Church will surely come only through the disciplined and creative fellowship of surrendered Christians; for such a fellowship in Christ is God's supreme weapon for the evangelization of the world (1 John 1:5-7 and John 17:22, 23). The isolated Christian is an anomaly.
—*Howard Guinness* in *Total Christian War.*

That which we have seen and heard declare we unto you, that ye also may have fellowship with us: and truly our fellowship is with the Father, and with his Son Jesus Christ. And these things write we unto you, that your joy may be full[1].—*the Apostle John*

And the multitude of them that believed were of one heart and of one soul: neither said any of them that ought of the things which he possessed was his own: but they had all things common.   —Acts 4:32

In World War II the United States narrowly escaped a crushing defeat because of neglect of a principle of war: the principle of cooperation.

Until the invasion of the Philippines, October 20-23, 1944, we had fought two separate wars in the Pacific: the advance through the Central Pacific, Gilbert, Marshall, and Mariana Islands, and the war in the Southwest Pacific via the Solomons and New Guinea. The forces of the former were commanded by Admiral Chester Nimitz in Hawaii and the latter by General Douglas MacArthur in Australia. When these advances met in the Philippines, the two leaders had no superior short of the Commander-in-Chief, the President of the United States.

The invasion was the responsibility of General MacArthur, with Central Pacific Forces filling a supporting role. The Seventh Fleet under the command of Vice Admiral Kincaid was given to General MacArthur for the invasion and included units of escort carriers and old battleships, some of which had been raised from Pearl Harbor. The ammunition of these units was non-armor-piercing, high explosive, as they were for support of the troops ashore and not for an engagement at sea.

Protecting the invasion from attack by sea was the Third Fleet commanded by Admiral Halsey under Admiral Nimitz. The main striking force consisted of four carrier air groups of four fast attack carriers each, and a surface striking force of new fast battleships.

The Japanese sent a two-pronged surface attack against the invasion fleet in Leyte Gulf and a decoy carrier group from Japan into the Philippine Sea. The old battleships under Rear

Admiral Oldendorf sank all but one cruiser in Surigao Strait, which took care of the southern prong. The fast attack carriers turned back the northern prong in the Sibuyan Sea and then proceeded after the decoy group away from the invasion fleet.

Because of poor communication between the commanders of the Third and Seventh Fleets, Admiral Kincaid thought that Admiral Halsey had detached his surface striking group of seven fast battleships to cover the northern prong of the Japanese surface force at San Bernardino Straits. In reality, Admiral Halsey took the battleships with him after the decoy air group. He had not let the Commander-in-Chief, Pacific, or Commander, Seventh Fleet know of his decision.

The Japanese northern arm returned to the attack, coming through San Bernardino Straits with four battleships and ten heavy cruisers. No one was there to meet them. They caught our escort carriers in Leyte Gulf. After sinking the *Gambier Bay*, for some unknown reason the Japanese admiral retreated. His only opposition consisted of torpedo attacks and smoke from destroyers and destroyer escorts.

Our forces had intelligence of the enemy. We had an overwhelming superiority in surface and air power. But we did not obtain a decisive victory because of poor communication between cooperating forces. If it had not been for the decision of the Japanese admiral to retire, we might have suffered a decisive defeat.

When we fail to uphold the principle of cooperation, we cannot count on the enemy making mistakes or poor decisions. Nor can we bank on scaring him with smoke and mock torpedo runs.

We must determine to have an overwhelming superiority to meet the enemy in a decisive battle at the right time, which cannot be achieved without cooperation.

Cooperation is dependent upon two prerequisites:

1. Cooperating forces are allies, not belligerents.

2. The cooperating forces come under one commander.

Cooperation with an enemy is not cooperation; it is treason. Failure to cooperate with an ally is a violation of an essential principle of war and a gross error.

Unity of command is necessary for cooperation. The closer the commander is to the cooperating forces, the closer the cooperation. The farther removed the unity of command, the weaker the cooperation.

In the invasion of the Philippines the supreme commander was very distant, the President of the United States. Admiral Nimitz had a unified command. So did General MacArthur. But this was a meeting of two distinct commands. They had no common superior close enough to the situation to provide good cooperation. The principle of cooperation is very important in the spiritual war.

First, it applies to each one of us individually. Most Christians are used to fighting (win or lose) their own spiritual battles. We are so used to fighting the spiritual war alone that when we come into contact with a fellow Christian in the same war at the same time or place, we find it difficult to cooperate and communicate. Cooperation is a prelude to concentration and concentration is one of the keys to victory.

It should be immediately apparent that the Christians have the advantage of a unified command. Furthermore, their Commander is not too far removed from the situation to provide effective cooperation. Jesus Christ himself experienced the temptations and difficulties encountered in this world, so he is close to our situation in the sense of personal experience.

More important, he presently occupies a position close to all Christians from which to direct their cooperative efforts—that is, he dwells in their hearts. From there he can guide us as individuals or as part of a group: "Where two or three are gathered together in my name, there am I in the midst of them" (Matthew 18:20). "I am with you alway, even unto the end of the world" (Matthew 28:20).

If there is any breakdown in the principle of cooperation, it is not on the part of the spiritual Commander; rather it must be traced to the individual combatants.

The greatest deterrent to cooperation is pride. Pride says I can handle my problems alone; I don't need any help. Or perhaps it will allow me to accept help, but not from *him!* Sometimes pride keeps us from admitting our needs even to ourselves, let alone to anyone else.

Other Christians could help us in our weakness, but we will not let them know what it is. A proud man wishes to win a struggle alone so he may take all the glory. When he loses no one else knows about it, or so he believes. James 5:16 says: "Confess your faults one to another, and pray one for another." This cooperation in the spiritual war is essential if we do not wish to be continually defeated at the point where pride hides the fault.

God's attitude toward pride is explicit in the Scriptures. Proverbs 6:16 says, "These six things doth the Lord hate . . . a *proud look* . . ." 1 John 2:15, 16 states, "Love not the world . . . For all that is in the world . . . the pride of life, is not of the Father, but is of the world."

The Bible also describes the results of pride. Daniel 5:20 explains the downfall of Nebuchadnezzar in these words: "But when his heart was lifted up, and his mind hardened in pride, he was deposed from his kingly throne, and they took his glory from him." King Uzziah suffered leprosy until the day of his death, because "when he was strong, his heart was lifted up" (2 Chronicles 26:16).

Proverbs 16:18 states the principle in this way: "Pride goeth before destruction, and an haughty spirit before a fall."

In the military services pride is deliberately generated in order to encourage obedience and high quality in performance of duties. Rivalry and competition in training bring the units to the peak of readiness.

Yet platoons should cease to compete when they act as a company. They are held together by the company commander. Companies should cease to compete when acting as a battalion and so on up the line until the Commander-in-Chief unites the Army, Navy, Air Force, and Marine Corps.

But a problem exists. Whereas the highest

sense of loyalty should be to the highest commander, the greatest pride somehow frequently is generated in the smaller units and the greatest loyalty is given to subordinate commanders. There may be fierce loyalty to the skipper and indifference, antagonism, or at best a lesser loyalty to the squadron commander. (This is no great difficulty as long as the skipper insures no deviation from orders by the squadron commander.)

Another way that pride is fostered is through the function of the unit. The method of warfare used in the particular unit becomes, so far as the men involved are concerned, the primary means of winning wars. For instance, the armor historian will tell the heroic part that that unit played in winning World War II. In turn, we can find out how destroyers, submarines, the Navy, the Air Force, Coast Guard, Marine Corps, and the Army each won the last war.

The pride and loyalty that is encouraged, the rivalry and competition that keeps units sharp and on their toes, can and does backfire. After a few years in the service, the naval officer has been indoctrinated to such an extent that it is difficult to cooperate with the Army, even though aims are in agreement. We then find that the individual thinks his loyalty to the Navy is synonymous with loyalty to the United States. Unfortunately, the Army feels the same way. Strained cooperation results. Thus the function of one's branch can become more important to an officer than the overall objective of the Armed Forces. This is a result of instilling pride in subordinate units to the neglect of emphasizing higher loyalties.

In the Army of the Lord the same error may occur. The different units (denominations, mission societies, and nondenominational groups) may develop a pride in the distinctives of their church or fellowship. The doctrines, liturgy, or methods that make a group distinctive are the points which are emphasized.

Many denominations and other groups are primarily the result of the ministry of individual men raised up by God: John Wesley, Martin Luther, John Calvin, Hudson Taylor, as well as living leaders. These are the "subordinate commanders" who may get the fierce loyalty and obedience which belong only to the Supreme Commander, Jesus Christ.

This would be strongly denied by most of us. Yet we betray our loyalties when our conversations frequently begin with ourselves or our group and its leader. Is Jesus Christ as often the subject of our opening sentences? If anyone draws this matter to our attention, we explain that our group and Christianity are synonymous, or that our leader is the most devoted follower of Jesus Christ, or that we meant Christianity, even if we did not say so. Thus each group feels it is most representative of Jesus Christ.

Strangely enough, if we were to apply the mathematical axiom, "Things equal to the same thing are equal to each other," we would conclude that all the groups were very nearly identical to each other and would enjoy great freedom in cooperation. This is not true. It is true that people who have a genuinely close fellowship and contact with the Supreme Commander have no trouble with each other, regardless of the groups with which they are associated.

We must guard our loyalty and keep it for the Lord Jesus Christ. "You shall love the Lord your God with all your heart, and with all your soul, and with all your mind. This is the great and first commandment. And a second is like it, You shall love your neighbor as yourself" (Matthew 22:37-39, RSV).

Sometimes we will encounter another Christian or Christian group on the same battlefield. Will we oppose his presence, tolerate his presence, ignore it, or unite with him to win the battle?

The question never really centers around the method of our group versus the method of the other group. The question is loyalty to our group versus loyalty to Jesus Christ. He commands both groups. For infantrymen not to accept the cooperation of tanks is not only stupid; it is disobedience to the one commander of both tanks and infantry. Our controversy is not with the other group—it is with Jesus Christ:

John said to him, "Teacher, we saw a man casting out demons in your name, and we forbade him because he was not following us." But Jesus said, "Do not forbid him; for no one who does a mighty work in my name will be able soon after to speak evil of me. For he that is not against us is for us" (Mark 9:38-40, RSV).

Our determining factor is the person of Jesus Christ. The man may not be with our group and we may disapprove of his methods. But if we agree with his loyalty to Jesus Christ and with his message, we should cooperate.

Paul saw this very clearly when he wrote:

> Some indeed preach Christ from envy and rivalry, but others from good will. The latter do it out of love, knowing that I am put here for the defense of the gospel; the former proclaim Christ out of partisanship, not sincerely but thinking to afflict me in my imprisonment. What then? Only that in every way, whether in pretense or in truth, Christ is proclaimed; and in that I rejoice (Philippians 1:15-18, RSV).

The other fellow's motives should not be our concern.

This is easy to say and to quote, but how to enter into an openhearted willingness to work with some one from another camp is not so easy. The problem is that we, as allied groups, are not close enough to the Supreme Commander, the Lord Jesus Christ. The solution, then, is to spend more time with Jesus Christ individually, in our group, and with other groups. This time alone or together should not be spent in thinking or talking about distinctives or differences. Nor should it be spent in accusation or introspection.

We should spend our time with him in prayer, praise, worship, reading, study, and meditation. When we listen to him, talk to him, sing praise to him and talk about him, we will come to know him better. We will begin to realize more of his love and power, and to follow more closely his commandments and purpose.

A new commandment I give to you, that you love one another; even as I have loved you, that you also love one another. By this all men will know that you are my disciples, if you have love for one another (John 13:34, 35, RSV).

QUESTIONS
1. Study 1 Corinthians 1:10-17 and 3:1-9.
2. Do you have a loyalty to a person, a doctrine, a group, or a name that hinders full cooperation with Christians with another loyalty?
3. If so, are you willing to admit that it is sin?

EIGHT
Communication

An Army marches on its stomach.
> —*Napoleon*

When your words came, I ate them; they
were my joy and my heart's delight, for I bear
your name, O Lord God Almighty.
> —Jeremiah 15:16, NIV

Napoleon expressed the principle of communication very well. He knew that a front line
army without food and ammunition cannot
fight or move, and invites defeat. Napoleon
himself lost two armies, one because he
neglected this principle, and the other because
the English severed his line of communication.

The official definition of "lines of communication" is: "All the routes, land, water and air,
which connect an operating military force with
its base of operations, along which supplies and
reinforcements move." [1] Adequate supplies must
continue to move along these routes until a
campaign is over. If an army is in pursuit, its
supplies must move all the faster and farther.
The principle of communications is violated
whenever an enemy is allowed to cut off
supplies or when an army advances too far and
too fast for adequate supplies to keep up.

Napoleon was defeated on both counts. In the

closing years of the eighteenth century he invaded Egypt. The French fleet in the Mediterranean provided the lines of communication. Militarily speaking, Egypt was an easy conquest. But the English got word of this movement and Lord Nelson went after the French fleet. He found and sunk it near the mouth of the Nile, stranding Napoleon's army in Egypt.

Years later, having conquered most of Europe, Napoleon invaded Russia. In the middle of winter he found he had disastrously overextended his line of supply. Another army was lost through violation of the principle of communication. It is no victory to defeat the enemy tactically and then freeze and starve to death.

In the fall and winter of 1950 the United Nations forces pursued their defeated enemy up the Korean peninsula faster than adequate food, winter clothing, ammunition, or engineers could follow. The victorious army arrived at the Yalu River thinned out in supplies and unprepared for winter. In this state they were caught by the Chinese Communist Army, which crossed the Yalu River supplied and winterized. The hitherto victorious army now retreated to the 38th parallel. Great numbers were overrun, surrounded, and captured. Only the amphibious evacuation at Hungnam saved most of a surrounded army. This principle of war may not be the most important, but it still must be practiced. Without it victory is temporary, defeat ultimate.

So it is in the war with Satan. Spiritual defeat is the only reward for those who overextend their lines of communication or allow them to be severed. We in the Army of the Lord must maintain communication with our Commander-in-Chief. He is the source of supply for spiritual food, ammunition, information, and orders. We have two-way communication with God: Prayer and the Word of God. Prayer is our means of communication to him. Via prayer we make our needs known; through intercession we ask help for cooperating forces. By prayer we praise him for victories won and confess our defeats.

In 1 Thessalonians 5:17 we are told to "pray constantly." Spiritual communication must not be broken. The enemy endeavors to cut our supply line by the simple device of temptation. If we yield, sin results, and sin severs. The presence of sin suppresses the desire to confess defeat. We do not praise God, thank him, or intercede for others. Confession is the only means of restoring communication.

God's means of communication with us is the Word of God. Any other spiritual communication is subject to test by this authoritative standard. He first spoke to men through the prophets and later through his Son and then through the apostles. We have these communications in the Bible, comprising all of our orders for the war with Satan.

But the Bible is more than that. It is our complete source of supply. It is our spiritual food. Job said, "I have esteemed the words of his mouth more than my necessary food" (Job 23:12). Jeremiah said, "Thy words were found, and I did eat them; and thy word was unto me the joy and rejoicing of mine heart: for I am

called by thy name, O Lord God of hosts"
(Jeremiah 15:16).

The Word of God is our weapon, "for the word of God is living and active, sharper than any two-edged sword, piercing to the division of soul and spirit, of joints and marrow, and discerning the thoughts and intentions of the heart" (Hebrews 4:12, RSV).

The Word of God is much more. By this means God develops faith, love, hope, and strength in us. In his Book he sets the standards of conduct. Through it he communicates his requirements of humility and absolute obedience, as well as many details and principles of the conduct of an army at war. He sets the bounds of fellowship among those within the camp and those without. As a weapon it is the most telling and effective in setting captives free from the power of Satan. "You have been born anew, not of perishable seed but of imperishable, through the living and abiding word of God" (1 Peter 1:23, RSV).

Even this portion of our two-way line of communication can be cut, and again it is sin that severs. With unconfessed sin in his life, the Christian has no desire to read, hear, study, or meditate upon the Word of God. He now neither communicates with God nor receives from him. It may have been a minor sin that severed the lines of communication; but once severed and not immediately restored, he is set up for a decisive defeat by Satan.

It is mandatory in the war with Satan that we have daily communication with our source of supply. We must receive daily from the Lord via the Word enough for all of the day's needs, and we must store up provisions of the Word of God in our hearts and heads for any future time when we have a prolonged engagement with Satan.

Daily time with the Lord is far more than our line of communication for the battle. Fellowship with him is really our objective. We were created and redeemed to walk with God. In fact, this is the reason why we are engaged in war, so that others may be brought into fellowship with him. "That which we have seen and heard declare we unto you [proclaim also to you], that ye also may have fellowship with us: and truly our fellowship is with the Father, and with his Son Jesus Christ" (1 John 1:3).

In Korea it seemed more important to implement the principle of war called pursuit than to keep in touch with supplies. This would have been right if the Chinese Communists had not entered the war. Our lines of communication can be overextended as well as cut. It may seem more important to be out witnessing or attending meetings than it is to spend time with our source of supply, the Lord Jesus Christ. Both witnessing and attending meetings are legitimate means of combating the enemy, but they cease to be effective when we run out of spiritual power. Scripture and sound military principle warn us that decisive defeat may be the end result. If we are fortunate, friends may be standing by to evacuate and keep us from defeat.

In Luke 10:38-42 is a story that illustrates this principle:

But Martha was distracted with much serving, and she went to him and said, "Lord, do you not care that my sister has left me to serve alone? Tell her then to help me." But the Lord answered her, "Martha, Martha, you are anxious and troubled about many things; one thing is needful. Mary has chosen the good portion, which shall not be taken away from her" (RSV).

Notice this: Martha was not far from the Lord nor was he far from her. The line of communication was short. Even though it was short she had still overextended herself. She had received nothing. She was too busy serving to receive. If we are too busy to spend time with the Lord, then we are too busy.

We are never far from him. The Second World War extended lines halfway around the world. We have not such a problem in distance for he said, "I am with you alway" (Matthew 28:20). We can pray to him at any time and place. We can receive from him through his Word all the supplies, strength, and wisdom needed for daily combat.

It is not the length of our lines of communication that is important—just the use of them!

QUESTIONS
  1. Study 1 Timothy 4:11-16.
  2. Do you have a time set aside daily to spend with God in Bible reading and prayer?
  3. Do you notice the difference in your life when you do not have this time with God?

4. Here are three booklets that might be a help to you in your quiet time: *Quiet time*, InterVarsity Press; *Manna in the Morning*, Stephen Olford, Moody Press; and *Seven Minutes with God*, The Navigators Press.

NINE
Economy of Force

The more the concentration can be
compressed into one act and one moment,
the more perfect are its results.—*Clausewitz*

And the three companies blew the
trumpets, and brake the pitchers, and held
the lamps in their left hands, and the
trumpets in their right hands to blow withal:
and they cried, The sword of the Lord, and of
Gideon. And they stood every man in his
place round about the camp: and all the host
ran, and cried, and fled.   —Judges 7:20, 21

Economy of force is efficiency in fighting,
effectiveness in warfare. If our objective is the
annihilation of the enemy army, we will take
the offensive at the decisive point. In order to
do this effectively, the combined application of
all principles of war is necessary. This
statement by General Erfurth mentions or
implies most of the principles of war:

To concentrate overwhelmingly superior
members at the decisive points is impossible
without strategic surprise. The assembly of
the shock-group must be done as quickly as
possible in such a way that all units can
attack at one and the same time.

Each of the following principles, when applied separately, economizes force. When they are applied in unison, economy of force is achieved. Let us look at each principle in the light of economy of force, realizing that all of them are interdependent:

1. Objective: The greatest incentive for economizing is to know where you are going and then go there.

2. Offense: "Going" economizes forces. It takes less force to mount an offense against one point than to defend all points.

3. Security: If the enemy does not know what we are going to do, we can do it with less force. If he knows, he will then be prepared and we may not be able to do it at all, even with a much greater force.

4. Surprise: This principle certainly allows a commander to do the job with less force.

5. Mobility: Mobility economizes force by increasing, in effect, the numbers of men and arms. "A leader who aims at mobility should not be afraid to strain his troops to the limit in order that they may reach the battlefield in time. Many victories were made possible by forced marches. Mobility equals increase in numbers" (Erfurth).

6. Cooperation: When allied forces advance with a common objective and in unity, they can attain victory with fewer men than if they had acted independently.

7. Concentration: This may seem to be, but is not, the opposite of economy of force. To use one's force in driblets here and there may only result in consistent defeat. But if we con-

centrate at the decisive points, we are using economy of force.

There is such a thing as overconcentration in places which are not decisive points. "Consequently, the fronts where no decisions are being sought should be manned with a minimum of force" (Erfurth). To concentrate at undecisive points violates economy of force. It is better to have one's force scattered in driblets at decisive points than have it concentrated at an undecisive point.

As we apply the various aspects of the principle of economy of force to the spiritual war in which we are engaged, we can say that any concentration of Christians where there are few or no non-Christians is an overconcentration at a point which is not decisive. To have a concentration of Christians where paganism is thick and rampant is compatible with the principles of war.

Because Christians have a tendency to concentrate at undecisive points, it may be difficult to get more than a few away from places of mislocated concentration to points where decisive battles are being fought. The few may not be enough for effective concentration, but their proper deployment is a step in the right direction, a step toward economy of force. Not to send a few to the decisive points would violate several principles of war. Economy of force uses what is available to do the job.

When there are many decisive points and the Christians are congregated away from the front, we ought to plead with God for economy of force: "And I sought for a man among them who should build up the wall and stand in the breach before me for the land, that I should not destroy it; but I found none" (Ezekiel 22:30, RSV).

Concentration in a noncombatant area is legitimate for training, to receive power or to prepare to attack. If concentration remains after training has been accomplished or if we dilly-dally around in the rear, we will never be ready for war. This is a waste of force!

The Lord Jesus Christ said to his disciples:

Thus it is written, that the Christ should suffer and on the third day rise from the dead, and that repentance and forgiveness of sins should be preached in his name to all nations, beginning from Jerusalem. You are witnesses of these things. And behold, I send the promise of my Father upon you; but stay in the city, until you are clothed with power from on high (Luke 24:46-49, RSV).

The primary objective was "all nations." Jerusalem was the place where power was to be received and from which the early believers were to start after they had received the power. However, they stayed in Jerusalem a prolonged period of time after the coming of the Holy Spirit at Pentecost. Their failure to move out was disobedience to orders. But God finally forced them to leave by allowing persecution. Concentration in the wrong place is not economy of force.

When these principles are combined with an

offensive at a decisive point, we are practicing economy of force.

In biblical history the greatest example of these principles combined in one military battle is Gideon's victory over the armies of Midian and Amalek described in Judges 7 and 8. In his God-directed use of economy of force, Gideon sent 31,700 men home and won the battle with 300 men.

The much-needed application of this principle is that we must send to the decisive points men who are willing and ready to go. It may be that, as it was with Gideon, 22,000 are afraid to go and another 9,700 are not ready to go. Thus, perhaps only 300 men are willing and ready to go with the message of Jesus Christ.

It was not God's plans to invite the Midianites and the Amalekites one and two at a time to the Israelites' home towns where the 31,700 soldiers could take them captive. Nor is it his plan to invite non-Christians one and two at a time into an overconcentration of Christians at an undecisive point where the believers preach the gospel at each other. It is God's plan to attack the decisive points with victory in mind. There are so many places and so few willing to go that we must economize our force.

Jesus said, "The harvest is plentiful, but the laborers are few; pray therefore the Lord of the harvest to send out laborers into his harvest" (Luke 10:2, RSV).

This is imperative. Jesus Christ tells us to pray that God would send men. He commands

us to do it and tells us why. The harvest is too
much for the few reapers. Let us pray for
economy of force.

QUESTIONS
  1. Study Judges 7.
  2. Are you *willing* to obey God even if the rest of
     the Christians are not *willing*?
  3. Are you *ready* to obey God even if the rest
     of the Christians are not *ready*?
  4. Will you obey God even if you are alone?

TEN
Pursuit

Only pursuit of the beaten enemy gives the fruits of victory.   —*Clausewitz*

Day after day, in the temple courts and from house to house, they never stopped teaching and proclaiming the good news that Jesus is the Christ.   —Acts 5:42, NIV

In his biography of Field Marshall Viscount Allenby of Megiddo and Felixstowe, General Sir Archibald Wavell, K.C.B., C.M.G., M.C., gives a very clear picture of the problems of pursuit:

> To the uninitiated, pursuit seems the easiest possible form of war. To chase a flying, presumably demoralized enemy must be a simple matter, promising much gain at the expense of some exertion and hardship, but little danger. Yet the successful or sustained pursuits of history have been few, the escapes from a lost battle many. The reasons are partly material, but mainly moral. A force retreating falls back on its depots and reinforcements; unless it is overrun, it is growing stronger all the time, and there are many expedients besides fighting by which it can gain time: bridges

or roads may be blown up, defiles blocked, supplies destroyed. The pursuer soon outruns his normal resources. He may possibly be able to feed himself at the expense of his enemies or of the countryside; he is not likely to replenish his ammunition and warlike equipment in the same way.

But the chief obstacle he has to overcome is psychological. The pursued has a greater incentive to haste than the pursuer, and, unless he is demoralized, a stronger urge to fight. It is only natural that the soldier who has risked his life and spent his toil in winning a battle should desire relaxation in safety as his meed of victory, and that the general and staff should feel a reaction from the strain. So that while coolness in disaster is the supreme proof of a Commander's courage, energy in pursuit is the surest test of his strength of will. Few have carried out pursuits with such relentless determination as Allenby in 1917 and 1918.

The spiritual war for men is not much different. If the principles of war were applied by a body of believers in any given locality, I believe there would be a great spiritual victory. The battle would be won and there would be many spiritual conversions to Jesus Christ.

However, once a breakthrough for Christ is achieved, we tend to relax, as though the fight were over.

Consider Gideon's rout of the Midianites. In Judges 7 we find that, for the battle, 300 men were all that were needed to make the breakthrough. But once the battle was won and the Midianites were fleeing, Gideon called for the men he had previously sent home; three of the four tribes joined in the pursuit. He also called out the tribe of Ephraim to cut off the fleeing Midianites by seizing the fords of the Jordan. "And Gideon came to the Jordan and passed over, he and the three hundred men who were with him, faint yet pursuing" (Judges 8:4, RSV).

The fact that 120,000 of the enemy were already slain, that Gideon had won the battle, and that he and his men were tired and hungry, did not stop his pursuit. By this time only fifteen thousand of the enemy remained. "And Gideon went up by the caravan route east of Nobah and Jogbehah, and attacked the army; for the army was off its guard. And Zebah and Zalmunna fled; and he pursued them and took the two kings of Midian, Zebah and Zalmunna, and he threw all of the army into a panic. Then Gideon . . . returned from the battle . . .".(vv. 11-13).

In physical warfare, the fruits of victory are conserved by pursuing the beaten enemy. The victors cannot relax or just "follow-up" the prisoners of war. The pursuit will bring many more prisoners in a short time, but if it is delayed, another major battle will ensue. The defeated enemy will have time to regroup his forces.

In spiritual warfare we must think beyond the converts made in the immediate battle. We must pursue the many non-Christians who are "fleeing" in conviction of sin, but who as yet have not surrendered to Jesus Christ. In other words, we as Christians ought to consider the principle of pursuit to be as important as "follow up" of the new Christians after a spiritual breakthrough. The victory has prepared many men almost to receive Jesus Christ.

Although it is very important to take care of prisoners of war, it takes a minimum of men to take care of disarmed prisoners. In spiritual warfare the prisoners are the converts to Jesus Christ. They are not only disarmed, they are now on our side. It should take fewer people to follow through on the new converts than is needed to pursue the great numbers who have been defeated but who have not yet surrendered to Jesus Christ. Sometimes after a major spiritual victory, "follow up" is not even attempted. Still worse is the failure to press the pursuit of those who are running away from Jesus Christ.

The most effective way to pursue the beaten enemy in physical war is to hit him from his unprotected flanks. If a direct pursuit is carried out, the victors run into the deadly sting of the rear guard and into many roadblocks and blown bridges, and so the retreating enemy gets away. To avoid these, the victors should travel a parallel path, outrun and intercept the retreating enemy. To continue direct pursuit after the battle is won is to lose the retreating enemy. In order to effect an interception in the pursuit, mobility is needed. If immediate pursuit is undertaken, as many more captives as were taken in the battle can be secured.

Prior to the Megiddo battle in September 1918, Allenby promised his cavalry 30,000 prisoners of war. His staff thought he was presumptuous. In reality he ended with 50,000 prisoners, having reduced the Turkish Seventh and Eighth armies to a few columns.

Let us consider the "how" of spiritual pursuit. First, we must be convinced that many people are ready to receive Christ and will receive him if they are cut off and confronted with their sin and the Savior. When a man begins to run away, he is ready to be captured. This does not mean that he will not put up a last desperate struggle or will not continue to run. This is why it is important to cut off his retreat.

To outrun fleeing, convicted sinners, God-directed mobility is required. As in Gideon's case, it might take a small, well-disciplined, courageous group to make a breakthrough in the spiritual conflict for men. Once the breakthrough has been made and many have received Christ, many others will have been convicted of sin, righteousness, and judgment and will begin to flee. Then we need more than our hard core of trained men. We need, like Gideon, all of the Christians who were not prepared for the battle but who are necessary in the pursuit. If we depend only on the hard core of Christians who seek to follow hard after Christ, we will win many battles, but there will be no complete rout. There will be successful evangelistic campaigns, but no awakening. If pursuit is practiced, every successful evangelistic campaign is a possible prelude to a general awakening.

If we study spiritual awakenings from Pentecost to the Welsh Revival of 1901 and the Korean revival of 1905, we notice the battle and the breakthrough centered around one man or a small group of men. This was only the start. After that, many Christians witnessed and testified of saving grace and more people were converted. Christians got right with the Lord and entered the chase. The whole church was in the awakening. Evan Roberts was not responsible for the 70,000 new Christians in Wales; he was only the leader. God's revivals may start with God-picked men. But they continue only if every Christian, weak or strong, joins in the pursuit.

It is the responsibility of the leader not only to make the breakthrough in the battle with his picked men, but also to call in all of the reserves for the rout. Our greatest mobility is in the quantity of Christians who can testify of the saving grace of Jesus Christ. At that time, every Christian should testify to everyone he meets.

Another means of mobility in pursuit is literature distribution—booklets, tracts, books, and Scripture portions—all of them on the judgment and love of God. The literature may be offered without charge and distributed at meetings, by the mass of Christians, or by direct mail.

A third factor essential to effective pursuit is the manner and content of our appeal. In preaching Christ to the people just prior to the breakthrough, it is possible to be somewhat removed from one's audience. But in pursuit we must be clearly identified with the people. Let there be compassion and understanding in our approach.

Furthermore, an ultimatum should be used in

our message, citing the judgment of God on unrepentant men. This is the only effective means that will cause a fleeing man to surrender to Christ. Judgment is the reality he cannot escape if he persists in fleeing from Christ and therefore it has great force in causing a fugitive to stop in his flight. Yet our warning should be given in love and joy.

The church in Thessalonica witnessed to their countrymen in the true sense of pursuit. True, they were not established Christians like those of Ephesus. They did not have two years of Bible school with Paul as the teacher. They had heard the gospel only three Sabbath days. Nevertheless, Paul writes to them a few weeks later:

> For from you sounded out the word of the Lord not only in Macedonia and Achaia, but also in every place your faith to God-ward is spread abroad; so that we need not to speak any thing.

Will we follow their example?
We must if we are to win!

QUESTIONS
1. Study Judges 8:1-21 and Acts 5:17-41.
2. When God gives you conversions, one or many, do you want to rest?
3. What determines whether you should spend time in following up your converts or continue in aggressive evangelism?

ELEVEN
Obedience

If ye love me, keep my commandments.[1]
—*the Lord Jesus Christ*

"Behold, to obey is better than sacrifice" (1 Samuel 15:22). King Saul had just won a battle of annihilation and now, because of disobedience, Samuel pronounces: "The Lord hath rejected thee from being king." Those are hard lines with which to meet a triumphant victorious king. It was a hollow victory and an empty triumph. Saul had tried to improve upon the commandment of God. We do the same today, only in more subtle ways.

There are certain words that command respect. They speak of something held in high regard. Few people hold a negative view of these words. One of them is *volunteer!* The sound of the word may cause shivers to run through a man. The word is used where ideals are at stake, where danger and death are the reward, where sacrifice is necessary. It has the sound of someone above the crowd—the exception; someone of a free will doing something with the consequences clearly in mind. The word occurs in time of war. It also applies to the spiritual war, especially in the foreign missions enterprise, as in the Student *Volunteer*

Movement of the early part of the twentieth century.

In recent months I have been asking groups of Christians a simple question. "Would you rather volunteer or would you rather obey?" With very few exceptions every group has responded overwhelmingly to volunteer.

The first time I asked this question was at a junior high Bible study group. Everybody wanted to volunteer. When asked why they would rather volunteer, the answer was clear. They got credit for volunteering and no credit at all for doing what they were told. One boy added some further insight into the problem. He was thinking about volunteering to clean the basement and was feeling rather fine about it when his mother cut his musing short with an order for him to clean the basement. She ruined it all! Suddenly he did not want to clean the basement. This question was prompted by the passage we were studying. Here it is in the New English Bible, Luke 17:7-10: "Suppose one of you has a servant ploughing or minding sheep. When he comes back from the fields, will the master say, 'Come along at once and sit down'? Will he not rather say, 'Prepare my supper, fasten your belt, and then wait on me while I have my meal; you can have yours afterwards'? Is he grateful to the servant for carrying out his orders? So with you: when you have carried out all your orders, you should say, 'We are servants and deserve no credit; we have only done our duty.'"

A word that occurs today with great frequency is the word *challenge*. Although it is not a synonym for *volunteer*, there is a close relationship between these words. If *challenge* is used as a synonym for *encourage* or *exhort*, no harm is done. But the word in today's vocabulary connotes the concept of the defiant challenger flinging down the gauntlet. This sort of challenge involves the application of subtle pressures on a man to attempt that which he previously has been either unwilling or unable to do. Often we hear Christian speakers portraying the difficulties and hazards of particular tasks in such a way as to provoke in the minds of their hearers a human pride that makes them eager to volunteer and do that which needs to be done.

The dictionary definition of "challenge" has a close resemblance to the word as we use it today, with one exception. We challenge our own team. According to the dictionary (Webster's New World), and according to tradition and history, a challenge comes from the enemy, the adversary, the sentry, the opposition. A challenge does not come from our team. It is defiance, a dare. Now with this definition we see the challenge occurring in Scripture. It first occurred subtly challenging God's authority, when the serpent said to the woman, "You shall not surely die." Other examples are (1) Satan's challenge to God to let him have access to Job in Job 1:9-11; 2:4, 5 (2) Goliath's defiance of the armies of Israel in 1 Samuel 17:10 (3) Elijah's challenge to the prophets of Baal on Mount Carmel in 1 Kings 18:21-27 and (4) Rabshakeh's famous challenge to the people on the wall to surrender in 2 Kings 18:27-37.

When the challenge comes from the enemy,

it may come as a threat, as a lie or a promise. In any case, it is an attempt to get us to respond on the *enemy's* conditions. The very nature of challenge is to lay out conditions determined by the challenger that the challenged must accept. If he is wise, the challenged will never respond to a challenge on the challenger's conditions.

There is a wonderful example in the New Testament of the enemy's challenge and the proper response: Acts 4:17-31. The apostles' response was *first* according to *God's* directive. "But Peter and John answered them: 'You yourselves judge which is right in God's sight, to obey you or to obey God. For we cannot stop speaking of what we ourselves have seen and heard'" (vv. 19, 20, TEV). They were then threatened *again*. The apostles' response to this second threatening was to present this challenge from the enemy to the Lord. "And now, Lord, take notice of the threats they made and allow us, your servants, to speak your message with all boldness" (v. 29). "When they finished praying, the place where they were meeting was shaken. They were all filled with the Holy Spirit and began to speak God's message with boldness" (v. 31). The apostles did not respond to the challenge in the flesh. They obeyed God and gained his power to be obedient.

Obedience is a willing or an unwilling carrying out of an order or a command. Most of our own experience from childhood up has been of the unwilling kind of obedience. This is one of the reasons "volunteer" has a better reputation than "obey." In our experience,

volunteering always means being willing.
Obedience always means to be unwilling. If,
however, we had known something of willing
obedience, then volunteering would be out
completely. God does not ask for volunteers,
nor does he challenge his own children. When
Jesus called his disciples he did the choosing.
He said, "Follow me." It was a simple imperative.
There were also a great many volunteers who
followed Jesus. The volunteers did not last.
Perhaps you think that volunteering is a greater
expression of love than obedience. What is your
basis? Jesus said, "If you love me you will obey
my commands," and "the man who has received
my commands and obeys them—he it is who
loves me" (John 14:15, 21, NEB). He made
simple, absolute, and authoritative statements.
These were not challenges seeking volunteers,
nor were they goals, landmarks to stretch our
reach, to make us try harder. They were imperatives of an absolute nature. Not to obey them
was sin. Every imperative from God since has
had an absoluteness in its nature and an un-
bendableness in its character that defies im-
provement of the commandment or satisfaction
if one falls short of the requirement.

In order to get men into the Armed Forces,
the Armed Forces put out recruiting posters.
"Join the Action Army," "Join the Navy and see
the world," "Let the world see you." These are
challenges to appeal to the pride of men so that
they will volunteer and join the Army.
However, once the man volunteers, the whole
system changes. He is no longer appealed to. He
is commanded and he obeys. The Army could
not command him into the Army, so they

used the challenge in order to get him to volunteer. Once he is in, it is a different story. Enlisting in the Army is the beginning of a command-obedience relationship. There is also an upper limit to this obedience, not as clearly defined as the enlistment at the beginning. In fact, it is always defined after the fact. For instance, an Army captain calls for his own position to be bombed with Napalm in order to destroy the enemy who has his company outnumbered and is overrunning his position. He receives the Silver Star and is recommended for the Congressional Medal of Honor for "danger above and beyond the call of duty." In the Army there is a beginning to obedience and there is a place above and beyond obedience. Between the lower limit and the upper limit the relationship is command-obedience.

Is there a lower limit to obedience in our relationship with God? There may be a lower limit in our ability to obey, but not a lower limit in the requirement to obey. This ability begins when we know Jesus Christ. In 1 John 2:3 we are told, "If we obey God's commands, then we are sure that we know him" (TEV). But before we knew Jesus Christ, we were under the command of God. And 1 Timothy 1:9 says, "It must be remembered, of course, that laws are made, not for good people, but for lawbreakers and criminals, for the godless and sinful, for those who are not religious or spiritual, for men who kill their fathers or mothers" (TEV). Even our repentance into life was commanded by God. In fact, it is a command to all men. Here it is in Paul's declaration at the University of Athens. "God has overlooked the times when men did not know, but now he commands all men everywhere to turn away from their evil ways" (Acts 17:30, TEV). No, God does not have a lower limit to obedience. He does not challenge us to volunteer for Christ. He commands all men everywhere to repent.

Is there an upper limit to obedience in the Christian life? Is there a "danger above and beyond the call of duty"? Can we volunteer beyond the highest command of God? What is the greatest command? Jesus said, "and thou shalt love the Lord thy God with all thy heart, and with all thy soul, and with all thy mind, and with all thy strength: this is the first commandment" (Mark 12:30). Now look at it again and see if by volunteering we can go beyond it. The superlatives are all there. God requires all of each of our faculties to love him. In Christian churches today it is normal to hear challenges to greater heights than *ever before*, but less of the commands.

Because the commandments of God are way beyond us—ideals which are not very realistic for the present—we make a graded scale and challenge Christians to follow the graded scale a step at a time. This is because we do not believe God provides the power and love and wisdom to obey his superlative commands as they are given. And since he does not provide, we decide we will dispense with the obedience, which is frustrating, and do it our way: challenge-volunteer. If we volunteer for less than the commandment requires, we are disobedient, even if we gain our objective.

There are many Christian works which are using the challenge today to get Christians supposedly to obey God in everything from Bible reading to the Great Commission. They are using it because it seems to work.

Christians are proud, too proud to obey. They will go to foreign mission fields because of a challenge presented in a dynamic way describing the lostness of the people, the dangers, and the hardships, whereas they will not go in obedience to a simple command given by Jesus Christ. A challenge is an appeal to the pride, to the ego of man. The challenge is doubly wrong. (1) It puts men on the foreign field who should be there, but it gets them there with a wrong motive. (2) It puts men there who should not be there.

There are men who have gone to the field in response to a challenge only to find it was obedience that could keep them there.

If we are not to challenge and we are not to volunteer and our only remembrance of obedience has been reluctant, recalcitrant obedience, how do we get so that we willingly obey? It all has to do with our view of the Commander. Do we worship him, stand in awe of him, love him, fear him, long to be with him? Or are we buddy-buddy with him? Do we think it is a 50-50 relationship? The latter is not love and will never get instant obedience. All of our obedience will be qualified, and therefore disobedience.

Now the end of the commandment is charity [love] out of a pure heart, and of a good conscience, and of faith unfeigned (1 Timothy 1:5).

If ye be willing and obedient, ye shall eat the good of the land (Isaiah 1:19).

QUESTIONS
1. Study Colossians 3:1-25.
2. List the imperatives in this chapter.
3. How many are there?
4. Is there a means of obedience as well as a requirement to obey?
5. Make a personal decision about each of these imperatives.

FOOTNOTES

Chapter 1. The Objective
1. 1 Corinthians 15:57, NIV.
2. Although the word "objective" is also an adjective, it will be used as a noun in this book, meaning the "objective point" or "mission."

Chapter 2. The Offensive
1. Luke 24:46, 47, NIV.
2. Hebrews 2:14, 15.
3. John 8:36.

Chapter 3. Concentration
1. Matthew 18:20, NIV.
2. "Git"—offensive; "thar"—objective; "fustest"—mobility; "mostest"—concentration.

Chapter 4. Mobility
1. 2 Timothy 2:9, NIV.
2. Under Admiral Halsey it was the Third Fleet. When Admiral Spruance was in command it was the Fifth Fleet.
3. 2 Timothy 2:9.

Chapter 5. Security
1. Ephesians 6:10-13.

Chapter 7. Cooperation
1. 1 John 1:3, 4.

Chapter 8. Communication
1. *Dictionary of U.S. Military Terms*, published by the Joint Chiefs of Staff, June 1948.

Chapter 11. Obedience
1. John 14:15.

NOTE FROM THE AUTHOR

To implement principles, methods are needed.
However, to use methods without understanding principles is to play into the enemy's
hands.

Since 1953 I have been studying and applying the principles of Christian warfare,
first personally and then with bodies of
believers. My associates and I are equipped
to teach the application of these principles.
You may write for information to:

> Mr. Jim Wilson
> Community Christian Ministries
> 125 East Third Street
> Moscow, Idaho 83843